When
Weakness
Becomes
Strength

Ghostwriter:
Laura Russell Simpson

WESTBOW
P R E S S®
A DIVISION OF THOMAS NELSON
& ZONDERVAN

Oak Tree image on cover created by Robert
O'Brien of Robert O'Brien Design

Scripture taken from the King James Version
or New King James Version of the Bible

WestBow Press books may be ordered through
booksellers or by contacting:

WestBow Press
A Division of Thomas Nelson & Zondervan
1663 Liberty Drive
Bloomington, IN 47403
www.westbowpress.com
1 (866) 928-1240

ISBN: 978-1-5127-3245-0 (sc)
ISBN: 978-1-5127-3246-7 (e)

Library of Congress Control Number: 2016903080

Print information available on the last page.

WestBow Press rev. date: 03/31/2016

The writings in this book are dedicated to the glory of Almighty God! May He be high and lifted up! And to the glory of His Son, Jesus Christ, the Saviour of the World! May He, too, be high and lifted up! And to the Holy Spirit, the spirit of the Living God, the One True God! The One who lives in those who are His and seals us to the day of redemption! The One who brings us to salvation, the One who teaches us the truths of God, the One who guides, comforts, and keeps us! And the One who reveals the Father to us!!! All praises be to The Father, Son and Holy Ghost!!!

Alleluia!!!

Laura Simpson   1-4-16

Acknowledgements

In thanksgiving to God for these whom He used to make this all happen! That is a book in itself!

To my husband, Bill, who has always encouraged me along this journey. To my daughter, Lauran, who also encouraged me, especially when times of discouragement would try to come in. God always gave her the words He knew I needed to hear. How I thank Him for her deep faith in Him, and her God given ability to recognize the enemy. To Bethany Strickland, at The UPS Store, whom God led me to knowing her heart for Him and her awesome willingness to do for me what He knew I could not do for myself. Only God knows how much I thank Him for her. There are no words I can speak to let her know how thankful

I am to Him for her part in this journey. To Marty Thomas, at Shepherds Fold Bookstore, whom God led me to in order to bring me to the divinely chosen publisher. Thank you, Lord, for Marty's willingness to help start the path to publishing. To all those at WestBow Press Publishing who helped to make this work of His happen. Thank You, Lord, for all the things they helped me to do, walking me through the path of publishing, a path of so many unknowns. To Elyse Jordan, a long time friend, with a special God given talent, whom God led me to make His vision for the cover designs happen. One who has such a sweet spirit and also a generous one, I thank you, Lord! You sent me to your best, Lord ! Thanks to all of you who have read and encouraged me through your words, sharing how God has blessed you as you have read His words. If you are blessed, then I am greatly blessed! Thank you, Lord, for these both family and friends! May You bless each of these for answering their call to help increase

Your kingdom, and to encourage and and teach each of us who are already Yours!!!

Alleluia!!!

Laura Simpson   1-4-16

To The Reader

II Corinthians 12: 9&10

and He said unto me, My grace is sufficient for thee: for My strength is made perfect in weakness. Most gladly therefore will I rather glory in my infirmities, that the power of Christ may rest upon me. Therefore I take pleasure in my infirmities, in reproaches, in necessities, in persecutions, in distresses for Christ's sake: for when I am weak, then I am strong.

It is through many years of personal experiences, struggles, and sufferings that God has brought forth this collection of writings. These are His words, not mine. Our sufferings are never wasted. Our weaknesses do become our strengths through His help. My prayer is that His words will encourage you, that He will reveal to you the times of weakness that made you strong, that you will see His presence with you as He carries you from your weaknesses to strength. May you experience His faithfulness to His words in II Corinthians 12:9&10.

Alleluia!!!

Laura Simpson   12-30-15

Psalm 40 My Song

I waited patiently for the Lord;
And He inclined to me,
And heard my cry.
He also brought me up out of a horrible pit,
Out of the miry clay,
And set my feet upon a rock,
And established my steps.
He has put a new song in my mouth –
Praise to our God;
Many will see it and fear,
And will trust in the Lord.

This psalm has become to me my story, and yes, my song. God has made it very personal for me. As I read it now, I see my life as it has unfolded. There were years and years, troubled years, of pits and prisons. Beginning with a childhood, which was one of living with alcoholism and violence, I fell into the first pit. For years I dealt with emotional scars. Through the following years there were many pits and prisons. There were pits of depression, anxieties, fears, which led to phobias, and panic attacks. Fear had such a grip on me that I was unable to drive for several years. In the meantime, I had been diagnosed with Bi-Polar disorder. For many years my life was a continual struggle. I had been saved in 1973, and through all my pits and prisons, I never doubted God's presence and care. With His help I never lost my faith in Him. When I would be hospitalized, I would always take my Bible. Many times I witnessed to others who had no hope, and to those who had not come to Christ as Savior and Lord. Like Joseph, I, too, knew He was always with me. He always carried me through. My pits were never too deep for Him. Interesting to note at this point, He gave me Psalm 40 each time I was in the hospital. I always knew, even in the struggles, He would bring me out. One day I knew Psalm 40 would be true for me. And so it has. This past Easter week God gave me a calling on my life. He had already begun my healing. I was no longer in the prison of bondage to fear. He, and He alone, had enabled me to drive again. My anxiety was leaving, there was no more depression, no panic attacks for years, and I began for the first time in many years to feel good. I realized that I was truly happy. I recognized that He was bringing me "out of the horrible pit". This time He had "set my feet upon a rock" and had "established my steps". He had put a "new song in my mouth". The calling to write His messages to me, to share with others, was my new song. Through what He has given me has brought praises to His great name. I have now written over thirty messages, and I make it very clear. The words I write are His words. I only put them on the paper. As I write and live a new life for Him, I pray the last verse of Psalm 40 will come to pass. My heart is His, and I pray He will use all He gives me to reach others for Christ. I want my life to count for Him. In the meantime, more healing has come. I have been healed from a stroke I had in 2014. It is no longer on the MRI. I am at this writing not diabetic. And now I am waiting and truly believing that He is going to heal my feet. I have no doubt this will come. Two weeks ago God gave me these scriptures in Job. In verses 16-19 of chapter 11 He spoke clearly to me of His healing my past.

vs. 16 Because you would forget your misery, and remember it as waters that have passed away,

vs. 17 And your life would be brighter than noonday. Though you were dark, you would be like morning

vs. 18 And you would be secure, because there is hope; Yes, you would dig about you, and take your rest in safety.

vs. 19 You would also lie down, and no one would make you afraid; Yes, many would court your favor. Then He took me to Isaiah 65:16 which says, So that he who blesses himself in the earth shall bless himself in the God of truth; And he who swears in the earth shall swear by the God of truth; Because the former troubles are forgotten, And because they are hidden from My eyes. I heard in these words He had healed me. Lastly, He gave me Job 13:27. It reads, You have set a limit for the soles of my feet. In this verse He was confirming to me the healing, which will come to my feet. I cannot thank Him or praise Him enough. Just like Joseph, He has been with me, too, through many years of pits and prisons. He never left me either. And again like Joseph, there was purpose in it all. And then again, too, there was like Joseph, an appointed time for God to bring me out. My appointed time has come. And how much I praise Him! Would I do it again? A definite Yes! All those years of struggles to bring me to this relationship with my Father and my Savior is oh, so, worth it. Each day now is His to answer His call – a call to share the love of God and the gospel message with all He puts in my path. Alleluia!!!

Laura Simpson   7-6-15

Always remember our sufferings are never wasted.

May the words of my mouth and the meditations of my heart be acceptable in Thy sight, O, Lord, this day.

This is the most important writing God has ever given me. It is a little long, but definitely worth the read. I do not make any apologies for His messages. I pray you will be blessed. The Message of the Cross and Beyond Laura Russell Simpson 8-10-15 From One Who Said "Yes". If you have a void in your life that you cannot seem to fill, or maybe you feel you have no purpose, or maybe you have lost hope; then I would like to tell you about One you may not know, who can answer all your needs. May I introduce you to the One I speak about? His name is Jesus. His gift is free to you, but not to Him. His gift to you cost Him His life. Did you know this Jesus loves you so much that He willingly died a horrible, shameful death on a wooden cross at a place called Calvary in order to provide a way for you to be forgiven for your sins? And before He was nailed to that cross, He was beaten beyond recognition. Blood ran down His head and face from a crown of thorns on His head. He was mocked and spit upon. Only vinegar and gall was offered Him to drink. The only thing He was guilty of was loving all people, healing and delivering multitudes, and revealing God, His Father, to a world who rejected Him. He hung there for hours before He died. And did you know He is the only way of salvation? For Jesus, Himself, said He is the Way, the Truth, and the Life. No man comes to the Father but by Him. (John 14:6) He tells you, if you believe there is any other way to heaven, then His death was in vain. His shed blood is the only way you can have forgiveness for your sins. He paid your penalty for you with His life. How great a love is that! If you want forgiveness for your sins, and an eternal home in heaven, and blessings beyond measure; then just pray a simple prayer. It does not have to be eloquent. First, admit to Him that you are a sinner. Confess your sins, and invite Him into your heart to live and reign as Savior and Lord. At that very moment His free gift is yours. And you only have to ask once. How easy is that? Then believe it by faith. If you have done this you have just entered into a wonderful relationship with the One True God. You now have God's very own Spirit living in you. It is the work of His Holy Spirit that will bring you blessings beyond measure. Your journey with Jesus has now begun. Once He has touched you, your life will never, ever, be the same. It will be truly an awesome experience. And it is the most important decision you will ever make. Your life beyond the Cross will bring these and more: joy unspeakable (1 Peter 1:8) healing (1 Peter 2:24) freedom (John 8:36) an exciting life (John 10:10) peace instead of anxiety (Phil 4:7) strength in weakness (2Cor12:9) love for others (Gal 5:22) hope (Rom15:13) guidance (Isaiah58:1) happiness (Prov16:20) help in times of affliction (Heb4:16) comfort (2Cor1:3&4) an eternal home in heaven (John 10:28) answered prayers (John 14:13&14) deliverance (2Chronicles20:17) wisdom and knowledge (Ephesians1:17) I want to close with this. None of us deserve what God gives us when we are saved. It truly is His grace.

As we walk in the power of His Holy Spirit, His grace will grow us. Our life in Him will truly be an abundant one. We just have to yield our hearts to Him daily. I tell you from my personal experience with Him, when He touched me, my life changed drastically. I simply must share with all the good news of His gospel message. This gospel message is not to be kept a secret. Alleluia!!! In His Great Love, Laura Simpson

One more comment about the scripture. It's all about our relationship with our Lord.

Thought for Today

Esteeming the Word of God

I cannot express to you how much importance I place on God's Word. Through His Word we know who He is, we know how He wants us to live, we know His way for our salvation through His Son, Jesus Christ. We know Him as the God of Genesis and the God of Revelation. We know all His many promises, what He tells us about prayer and how He feels about sin. The Bible is our manual to live by.

In Matthew 4:4 Jesus Himself says, It is written, Man shall not live by bread alone, but by every word that proceedeth out of the mouth of God. Notice here Jesus says it is written. And remember, too, Jesus is the Living Word. Needless to say here how important it is for each of us to read God's

Word, and not just read it but hear His words to us. There is a difference.

In Job 23:12 He says, I have esteemed the words of His mouth more than my necessary food.

The New Testament is full of scriptures which speak of the Word. Take time and look up these. You will learn a lot. But for now I want to share a passage in Nehemiah that God led me to. It has blessed me greatly and taught me so much! It has really touched me. I hope it will touch you, too. It's taken from Nehemiah 8. Because of length I will give the verses which are so special. All God's people have gathered together in the street and have asked Ezra, the scribe and priest, to bring the Book of the Law of Moses, which the Lord had commanded to Israel. (Verse 1) So in the beginning the Word was given to God's people and that means us. Ezra brings the Book of the Law before the congregation and before all that could hear with understanding. (Verse 2) He read in the street from morning until midday. And it says the ears of all the people were attentive. (Verse 3) They made a pulpit of wood, which Ezra stood upon. (Verse 4) Standing above the people on the pulpit, Ezra opens the Book, and when he does all the people stand up. (Verse 5) He then blesses the Lord, the great God. And listen to this. All the people answered, Amen, Amen. They lift up their hands, bow their heads, and worship the Lord with their faces to the ground. (Verse 6) How is that for esteeming God's Word and worshipping the One who gave it! Humbling themselves and on their faces before Almighty God! There's a lesson here for us in this one verse. Then in Verses 7&8 there were men who explained the Word to the congregation. Another awesome statement in Verse 9. Nehemiah, Ezra, and the Levites, who taught the people declared the day holy unto the Lord God. Listen to this. The people wept when they heard the words of the Law. Is that not incredible? Talk about esteeming His words! And maybe, too, they were under conviction. In verse 10 they were told to go, eat the fat, drink the sweet, be not sorry for the day was holy; for the joy of the Lord is your strength! After they had heard the Word and had bowed down in worship, they were instructed to go and celebrate. I truly believe that at this time God had addressed their sins, which brought them on their faces in repentance and on to forgiveness. I also believe this forgiveness led to their celebration and great joy. It is this joy of the Lord which gives us strength, just as it did them. In verse 11 God seems to be saying, do not grieve, your sins are forgiven. Now rejoice! Verse 12 says, they went forth celebrating because they understood the words that were declared unto them. Do you hear it? Celebrating God's Word! What a lesson for us to today! And again, esteeming God's Word!!! Oh friends, how much we fail in not heeding the lessons in this passage! Look at how much we miss when we fail to read our bibles each day. We miss God, Himself!!!

Alleluia!!!

Laura Russell Simpson

On The Ultimate Deliverance

There are many examples of deliverance in God's Word. In II Samuel 22 David literally stands back and watches as God delivers him from the hand of Saul and his enemies. If you have not read the lesson He gave me on this passage, go back and read it. It is awesome to hear David's words as he describes the account. Then in II Chronicles 20 God delivers King Jehoshaphat, Judah, and Jerusalem from their enemies. In this account God again says to His people to stand still and see the salvation of the Lord. There are several things to note in these examples. First there is deliverance. Second, it is God who delivers, not the people. Third, God provides the way of deliverance. II Chronicles 20:17 says, Ye shall not need to fight in this battle: set yourselves, stand ye still, and see the salvation of the Lord with you, O Judah and Jerusalem: fear not, nor be dismayed; tomorrow go out against them; for the Lord will be with you. In this verse He gives instructions for them as He delivers them. Fourth, there is an enemy. Moving on to the New Testament there are many examples given where Jesus delivers. In IITimothy 3:11 Paul speaks of being delivered. Then in Matthew 8:28-34 Jesus delivers the demoniac at Gadara. Same things to note here. There is an enemy, it is Jesus who delivers, it is accomplished His way, and a person cannot deliver himself. Here we come to the ultimate deliverance. Each one of us has the same enemy. His name is Satan. God has provided a way of deliverance for all. His way leads to an old rugged cross at a place called Calvary. On that cross He gave His only begotten Son to die a horrendous death, beaten beyond recognition, spit upon, nailed to that cross by His hands and feet, a crown of thorns on His head, blood running down His royal face, with His lifeblood pouring to that Holy ground. The greatest sacrifice ever given, by a God who loves you and me so much that He wanted to deliver each one of us from the enemy of our souls. He knew that we could not deliver ourselves, so He made a way for us. His way comes only through the shed blood of His Son, Jesus Christ. And His way is the only way. With this, too, we have instructions from our Father for our deliverance. Each one of us must come to that cross, we must admit that we are sinners in need of a Savior, we must bow before Him in repentance, we must ask this Jesus into our hearts, we must make Him our Savior and our Lord, and then receive by faith our deliverance from eternal damnation. When we do this, God then makes us His children and promises us eternal life with Him in heaven. Our name is then written in the Lamb's Book of Life. Friends, it can get no better than this! And do not forget this is our God and Father's gift to us! We only have to reach up and accept it as our own! His instructions also include giving us a choice. Our decision determines our eternal destiny. And that, my friends, is forever! I ask you now, if you have not been delivered by the shed blood of Jesus Christ, inviting Him into you heart as Savior and Lord, repenting of your sins, and asking for His forgiveness, then I urge you to come to Him now. He died for you! Don't make His death in vain. By rejecting Jesus as God's only way of deliverance, you do just that! His was the ultimate sacrifice, His very life, for yours! Think about how much He loves you! Invite Him into your life and you will never be the same again! Your journey with Him will take you places you've never been, show you things you've never seen, give you joy beyond belief, and give you fulfillment you've always yearned for! I conclude this with my testimony that all this He has given me to write is truth. I have made my choice, and that choice is Jesus Christ. He has changed my life, and never, never would I choose the other way! How I thank Him for loving me enough to give His life so that I might live!!! And living I am!!! Alleluia!!!

Laura Russell Simpson

Thought For Today

To All My Friends And Family

Let's all join in together tomorrow in a chorus of praise and thanksgiving to God for all His goodness to us, especially the gift of the Savior of the world!!! The ultimate reason to give thanks on this special day!!!

Alleluia!!!

Laura Simpson   11-25-15

From My Heart

Another Thought On Our Journey

From my own personal experiences I want to share this with you. From our times of struggles and sufferings, hardships our weakness will become our strength! I know this is true because I would never be where I am today if it had not been because of the times I have struggled. And like He said through a recent message, He is not in a hurry. It took years to bring me to the place where I can truly say, The joy of the Lord is my strength! I can look back and see that these were years of preparation. The same is true for you. We all must learn to give thanks in all things. When He puts us in a hard place we must see it as His evidence of His hand at work in our lives. When we truly grasp this, we can truly give thanks. And we can experience joy, in spite of our circumstances. And it is through the work of His Holy Spirit that He works in each of us to make it all happen. Look back over your life and see if you can recognize the times when you felt weak and see if you, too, can say that this weakness has become your strength. Pray and ask your Father to show you this. He will use this greatly to encourage you as you continue on your journey with Jesus!!! May the joy of our Lord be your strength, too!!!

Alleluia!!!

Laura Simpson   12-26-15

Thought for The Day

This is the day the Lord has made. I will greatly rejoice and be glad in it. This day is Yours. Wherever You lead I will follow.

Thought For Today

Let's all remember that this day over two thousand years ago Jesus had begun His journey to the cross. And it would not be an easy one! And our journey is not an easy one either. But because of His going before us even unto His death, our journey is not alone. He has already walked where we have to walk. He knows our weaknesses, our infirmities, our struggles, our fears, our pain, our suffering. And our journey is His, too, right beside us all the way. Let Him help you! When we hurt, He hurts, too. When we are joyful, He is, too. Whatever the need, He is there with us. His shed blood has a power in it that we cannot comprehend. When we have been covered by His blood, we will experience this power oftentimes when we are not even aware of it. This is why His word says that by His stripes we are healed. And there are many kinds of healing. There is truly a mystery in the shed blood of Jesus Christ, our Savior and our Lord! God in His sovereignty does not choose to reveal all things to us. Nevertheless, His truth is truth! There is a song by Robin Herd in which he sings, through the fire, through the flood, you are covered by The Blood; for I am with thee! What beautiful words. Let them minister to you and to me this day!!!

Alleluia!!!

Laura Simpson   12-26-15

I love you, all!

Another Thought
On Christmas

This message is for anyone who is reading it that may be depressed, discouraged, despairing, or feeling hopeless. Fight it with faith! And don't say you have no faith or not enough faith! God's Word says He gives everyone a measure of faith. And Jesus said it only takes faith the size of a mustard seed. That mustard seed grows into a tree when fertilized with the Word of God! Don't give it up! And He says, don't give it up to the enemy of your soul! Your enemy and mine seeks to kill, to steal, and to destroy you and me! Take it back from your enemy! Refuse the thoughts of despair and discouragement. Start praising God, even if you don't feel like praising Him! As you praise Him, His Holy Spirit will provide the feelings.

Depression, discouragement, despair, and hopelessness come from our enemy, NOT from our loving Father and our Savior, Jesus Christ! I can tell you these things because I have been there! And even before I was saved, God was carrying me. He has delivered me from the grips of our enemy. And He is waiting now, at this very moment, to help you! The sacrifice Jesus made for you and me on the cross by His death brings us eternal life, but His death brings us abundant life also! And that is available to you now. If you feel hopeless in your circumstances, hear what God is saying to you! David said, why art thou cast down, oh, my soul. Hope thou in God! Jesus's death, His shed blood, gives us hope eternal! Look to Him. He will provide hope for you! He will deliver you. David stood back and watched as God delivered him from his enemies. So did Gideon, not to mention His deliverance of His people out of Egypt! He knows we cannot deliver ourselves. That's why He gave us His Son, who delivers us by His shed blood! My friends, that is HOPE! And if you need healing, remember, as the post today says, God is Jehovah-Rapha, the Lord that healeth! That is written in His Word as the second name of God out of seven names given. And the Word also says that by the stripes Jesus took, we are healed! Yes, He does not always heal, but often He does. I know, because He has healed me. There is a power in the shed blood of Jesus that goes deeper than what our finite minds can comprehend. Only God knows this power. It is His! He is omnipotent! Lastly, if you have not come to Christ for forgiveness and cleansing only by His shed blood, and given Him your heart, I urge you to do it now! Receive Him as Savior and Lord. And get ready!!! You will never be the same again!!! Alleluia!!!

Laura Simpson   12-19-15

Message For Today

Last night the Lord spoke to me and impressed upon me to post this message today. There are some who read this that are in circumstances where you're waiting on God for reasons only you know. And it is difficult for you. The message is that God does not hurry! All through His Word we see this truth. For this reason He desires for me to post again a message He gave me dated 8-8-15. Isaiah 40:31 says, But those who wait on the Lord shall renew their strength; they shall mount up with wings like eagles, they shall run and not be weary, they shall walk and not faint. Job 14:14-16 says, If a man dies, shall he live again? All the days of my hard service I will wait, till my change comes. You shall call, and I will answer you; you shall desire the work of your hands, for now you number my steps,..... Lamentations 3:25-32 says, the Lord is good to those who wait for Him, to the soul who seeks Him. It is good that one should hope and wait quietly for the salvation of the Lord. It is good for a man to bear the yoke in his youth. Let him sit alone and keep silent, because God has laid it on him; let him put his mouth in the dust--- there may yet be hope. Let him give his cheek to the one who strikes him, and be full of reproach. For the Lord will not cast off forever. Though He causes grief, yet He will show compassion according to the multitude of His mercies. Verse 38 says, Is it not from the mouth of the Most High that woe and well-being proceed? In Isaiah 40:31 Isaiah speaks of those who wait on the Lord. I ask, "wait for what?" What I hear in waiting is giving God time to work out His purposes in our lives. Remember, He orders our steps and fashions our days. During our times of waiting, we can rest knowing that a time will come when His purposes are accomplished. Also, as we wait, we must trust. Then look what He offers us-- a renewed strength, the strength of eagle wings. We can run and not be weary and walk and not faint all because we have had a time of rest while we waited. Going back to Psalm 40, David said he waited patiently for the Lord. He goes on to reveal this as a time of prayer. In these verses I hear that David was not striving, but resting and praying. Just look at what God was doing in David's life during this time. Do go back and read Psalm 40 again. It, too, speaks to us of a time when God was hard at work, working out His purposes and ultimately bringing David to an awesome place where He would use him greatly. In Job 14:14-16 we see the same principals. Job is in a hard place, a time of affliction; but he, too, says, I will wait till my change comes. Can't you just hear his patience and trust in the Lord? He, too, reveals it as a time of prayer; and he also sees how God is ordering his steps as he waits. Job's faith shines through these passages. Then in Lamentations 3:25-32 Jeremiah, who is believed to be the author of this book, speaks of how good God is to those who wait for Him. I see in this how the Lord rewards our faith and trust in Him as we, too, cease our striving and give Him time to work His purposes in our lives. Verse 26 calls us to wait quietly for His help. Jeremiah adds how good it is for us during these times of affliction. He says, sit alone and keep silent. He says no complaining or blaming. God is at work. Verse 31 tells us that these times are not forever. And lastly in verse 32, even though God allows these times, as Jeremiah puts it, times of grief, yet our Father will show compassion, revealing to us the multitude of His mercies. So once again we see in these passages a call to wait on the Lord in patience, rest, quietness, and trust. Also these are times we are called to prayer as we allow our God to work in our lives as He brings us out rested and strong to that wonderful place that only He can achieve. Just look at the final result. It is a place where He will use us to touch others (Psalm 40:3).

For those who need to hear this message today, my prayers are with you.

Showing us the way!!!

Alleluia!!!

Laura Simpson   12-17-15

Thought For Today

The Lord has called me to share these words from Him today. There are those of you who have lost loved ones during the past year, some recently, some we maybe still grieve for. The Christmas season can be very difficult and very emotional when we arc grieving. He gave me this passage to share with you, and in it He tells us how to get through our grief. Hear Him speak as He reaches out to comfort you

Isaiah 61:3 .... To give unto them beauty for ashes, the oil of joy for mourning, the garment of praise for the spirit of heaviness; that they might be called trees of righteousness, the planting of the Lord, that He might be glorified.

I offer to you this beautiful passage as you mourn your loss. May these words comfort you and strengthen you as you read them and hear God's own voice as He speaks to you personally. Instead of ashes (death) He is offering you beauty, a beauty that your loved one possessed, the beauty of a life that touched you and many others. He offers you the beauty of their memory, and the love they had for you and others. Our Lord offers you, too, the oil of joy for mourning. As you mourn, He will give you His joy to soothe and comfort you. The oil speaks of the work of the Holy Spirit in comforting you. Remember His words which say that the joy of the Lord is our strength. His Spirit will strengthen you as you look to Him. He calls you to clothe yourself with praise when your spirit is heavy with your loss. He knows and is reminding you of how powerful praise is. Praises to the God of comfort will lift your spirits and bring healing to your hearts. In doing this, the Lord is likening you to a tree. A tree He has planted strong with roots that go deep, a tree that can weather the storms that you face. You are like a tree that provides shade to those He calls you to help comfort, those who walk this path also. He calls you to share these, His words, with those who may not know Him and the comfort He brings. And in all this He is glorified!!! You have the privilege of bringing glory to His name! Once again we hear His love flow through His words to us, reaching out to show us the way!!!

Alleluia!!!

Laura Simpson   12-10-15

Thought for Today

Ecclesiastes 3:14. I know that, whatsoever God doeth, it shall be forever: nothing can be put to it, nor anything taken from it: and God doeth it, that men should fear before Him.

Thought For Today

Isaiah 26:3&4

Thou wilt keep him in perfect peace, whose mind is stayed on Thee: because he trusteth in Thee. Trust ye in the Lord forever: for in the Lord JEHOVAH is everlasting strength.

It's all about our focus. And it's also about our choice. Our choice is either the way of peace or the way of worry. We either choose to focus on God, or we choose to focus on our circumstances. If our choice is God then we have peace as we trust Him with our circumstances. He says in these verses that if our mind is stayed on Him, we will have perfect peace. Stayed on Him means fixed on Him. To me it speaks of firmly on Him. And He alone can give perfect peace. Remember His words, perfect love casts out fear. These words fit so well with focusing on Him as we trust Him with our circumstances. As we trust Him we are not fearful. Here we experience His great love once again. He's showing us the way of peace, perfect peace. Our other choice is to focus on our circumstances. If we do this, it will always lead to worry, defeat, despair, anxiety, failure, and on and on. And there is no peace at all in this choice. Therefore, if we find ourselves overcome with worry, anxiety and the like, then we must turn our eyes to God; confess our failure to trust Him, and consciously make the choice to focus on Him. Through these words He shows us the way again. Again I say, can't you just hear His love in them? What a wonderful Father He is!!!

Alleluia!!!

Laura Simpson   12-9-15

Thought For Today

Philippians 4:6&7

Be anxious for nothing; but in everything by prayer and supplication with thanksgiving let your requests be made known to God. And the peace of God, which surpasses all understanding, shall guard your hearts and minds through Christ Jesus.

This is a verse we are all familiar with. With the events of our world and the events of our lives, we all face anxiety everyday. Stress. Just the mention of that word causes my mind and body to tighten up. There seems to be a force behind it. And actually, there is. It comes from the enemy of our souls, the one who seeks our hurt any way he can make that happen. And we all know that anxiety/stress breaks our health down. God tells us He (our enemy) comes to steal, kill, and destroy. We don't have to look far to see in our own lives or those we love the truth of God's words. Here's the good news. God knew we would deal with anxiety and that we would need His divine help to overcome it in our lives. So, in these verses He instructs us. Remember first of all that anxiety is a lack of faith on our part. If we are anxious about anything, we are not trusting Him with the circumstances which are creating it. Our enemy sneaks in our thoughts and if we don't reject him, we will live in defeat. But God tells us we can have His supernatural peace, His peace which surpasses all of our human understanding. Sounds great to me! What about you? It is miserable living in the grips of stress/anxiety. How awesome to be able to have God's peace instead. Verse 6 tells us how that will happen. Through prayer and supplication tell God you need His help. Tell Him you cannot do this on your own. Ask His forgiveness for your lack of faith. Resist the enemy of your soul, resisting in the Name above all Names, the Lord Jesus Christ. Tell God you want to give Him your anxiety in exchange for His supernatural peace. Don't forget to thank Him for His words that again show us the way of victory. Thank Him for His faithfulness to His words. And friends, above all, remember the victory is already ours. As Jesus shed His blood on the cross, He won the victory over sin and death! And that same victory is already ours! Let's not let our enemy steal what is already ours by the finished work of Christ on the cross! Before closing, I want to share what God has shown me in these verses. He revealed a new way to pray this scripture. I had never seen this before. Verse 7 says His peace will guard our hearts and minds in Christ Jesus. He revealed to me that in praying about our hearts, we can ask Him to not only guard the spiritual things of our hearts, but also the physical. Pray for His peace to guard against heart attacks and heart problems. Then in praying for His peace to guard our minds, not only for our thoughts, but also pray against strokes, aneurysms, and brain diseases. What is so intriguing to me is the connection between anxiety and health problems. And also how His peace guards us from these problems. All, as the verse says, is through Christ Jesus!!! He truly holds the answers to all our needs! Once again the victory is already ours. Sin no longer has dominion over us! Help us, Lord, to not be deceived by the enemy of our souls! Help us to walk in your peace and freedom!

Alleluia!!!

Laura Simpson   11-21-15

Thought For Today

God Still Moves Mountains

Zechariah 4:6&7

Then He answered and spake unto me, saying, This is the Word of the Lord unto Zerubbabel, saying, Not by might, nor by power, but by my spirit, saith the Lord of hosts. Who art thou, O great mountain? Before Zerubbabel thou shalt become a plain: and he shall bring forth the headstone thereof with shoutings, crying, Grace, grace unto it. The last message was on God's forgiveness for us. In this message today He is addressing our unforgiveness for those who have hurt or offended us. His words are extremely important in this lesson. Please keep reading! In these scriptures Zerubbabel was facing a mountain. God speaks to the mountain and says, who are you, O great mountain? He tells Zerubbabel that it will become a plain before him. He also tells Zerubbabel that it will not be by power, for he has none, nor by might, for he has none either, but by the Spirit of the Lord of hosts that it will come down. Then He says in the process shall come forth the headstone with shoutings of Grace, Grace unto it. God is speaking of the headstone being Jesus. And look at the next words, Grace, Grace! I never knew that God's grace was mentioned in the Old Testament until I read this passage. Is this not awesome? We know that God's Grace came to us with the giving of His Son for the forgiveness of our sins. Look now at what He says about our unforgiveness for those who have hurt us. I venture to say, if you're like me, unforgiveness has built over the years until it has become a mountain before me. I pray this day that these mountains we each face will come down. Right now, as we read, God is speaking to our mountains, just as He did for Zerubbabel. He is telling us that, also like Zerubbabel, we have no power and no might of our own, but by His Spirit our mountain will come down, today if we hear His voice. God knows we cannot do this on our own. I have tried many times and always failed. Only by His Spirit! Holding onto our hurts and offences causes great pain and bitterness among other things. I don't know about you, but I'm more than ready to watch Him bring my mountain down! Unforgiveness is a bondage. And important to remember here are God's words, He cannot forgive us until we forgive others. Here enters His Grace. He has given us His Son and His shed blood on the cross to provide a way for us to not only be forgiven, but as a way to help us forgive others. God wants desperately to free us from our bondage to unforgiveness of others. He tells us that whom the Son sets free is free indeed! The shedding of the blood of Jesus is the way of freedom. What I want to point out here is that this has already been accomplished. We have been forgiven by His shed blood, but beyond that His shed blood provides a way for us to also forgive others. He is telling us here that we just need to receive His forgiveness, and watch His Holy Spirit bring down our mountain right before our eyes, just as He did for Zerubbabel. And His Grace will fall upon us in a mighty way! Again, He will do for us what we cannot do for ourselves. He loves us just that much! He is waiting patiently for us to ask His help and want to be freed from the bondage of unforgiveness. When we do this in obedience to Him, we can move on to greater things He has for us to do in complete freedom. In choosing not to forgive others God cannot forgive us, and we will not be able to continue in the journey He has planned for us. That choice will stall our walk with the One who yearns to free us! May this be the day for each of us to watch the Holy Spirit bring our mountain down and set us free!!! And we, too, will be shouting Grace, Grace just like Zerubbabel did in his moment!!!

Alleluia!!!

Laura Simpson   11-6-15

Thought for Today

About Faith

Out of difficult circumstances God speaks to us about our faith. Remember, faith is believing when we cannot see. It is trusting God no matter how things may appear. Those very things He can change in the blink of an eye! What we can see is limited at best. And faith is action. Believing and trusting is action! We must not be overcome by our circumstances and give up. This is our call by God to act! Get up, start walking, keep walking, put our faith into action! Trust God and believe Him to see us through our difficulties! Along the way talk to Him. If your faith is weak tell Him. He will increase it. And remember, it only takes faith the size of a mustard seed. Jesus said we could move mountains by faith. And that, friends, is action! If you are afraid tell Him. Tell Him whatever needs you have. We must recognize that our Father and Savior are right there with us! By faith believe this to be true. He says He will never leave us or forsake us! He walks our journey with us. As we keep walking, wait patiently remembering this is a time when He is strengthening us and giving us rest. As we wait, we must trust Him. All this time He is working out His purpose and plans for us. And be assured, His plans are for our good! He always rewards our faith and trust in Him! Faith Always Brings Results! We see this throughout the Bible! When you talk to Him, speak to Him as your Father. You are His child if you have given your life to Jesus Christ. And as your Heavenly Father, also like your earthly father, He will give you all things that are good for you out of His great love for you. He will even surprise you with things that you are not expecting. He delights in you! And He delights in knowing that you recognize His presence with you, that you trust Him to take care of you, that you believe

Him and His words to you. Thank Him this day if you know you are His child. Thank Him for walking with you whatever your journey. Thank Him that you know He will see you through no matter how circumstances may appear. Thank Him for being a Father and God and Savior you know you can trust! And do something in return for His love for you. Tell Him how much you love Him!!! By faith look into heaven and see His face as He responds to your words!!! As I look, I see tears of joy streaming down my Father's face!!! Awesome! Truly awesome!!!

Alleluia!!!   10-24-15

He says, you can talk it, or you can walk it! No sooner He gives me the message on focus than He puts my faith to the test! Well, with His help I'm going to walk it! It's difficult at times, but again, I say, with His help I will keep my focus on Him!!! I'm going to disappoint the enemy big time!!!

Alleluia!!! ♥ ♥ ♥

Thought for Today

Matthew 21:21-22

Jesus answered and said unto them, Verily I say unto you, If ye have faith, and doubt not, ye shall not only do this which is done to the fig tree, but also if ye shall say unto this mountain, Be thou removed, and be thou cast into the sea; it shall be done. And all things, whatsoever ye shall ask in prayer, believing, ye shall receive.

4 steps: ask, believe, doubt not, then receive!

One more thought on this scripture

I heard a preacher say that God is sitting on the edge of His throne saying, Ask Me for something big. Don't just ask Me to water your grass and feed your parakeet. Just look at all of His promises. He wants to prove Himself faithful to these promises. He gives us this scripture to show us how to receive His answers. He truly wants us to live in victory, not defeat! Our vision of our Heavenly Father can get so distorted sometimes. Alleluia!!!

Thought for Today

Acts 7:54-60

When they heard these things, they were cut to the heart, and they gnashed on him with their teeth. But he, being full of the Holy Ghost, looked up steadfastly into heaven, and saw the glory of God, and Jesus standing on the right hand of God, And said, Behold, I see the heavens opened, and the Son of man standing on the right hand of God. Then they cried out with a loud voice, and stopped their ears, and ran upon him with one accord, And cast him out of the city, and stoned him: and the witnesses laid down their clothes at a young man's feet, whose name was Saul. And they stoned Stephen, calling upon God, and saying, Lord Jesus, receive my spirit. And he kneeled down, and cried with a loud voice, Lord, lay not this sin to their charge. And when he had said this, he fell asleep.

Comment: This is the account of the stoning of Stephen, the first martyr. The purpose of this writing is to reveal how the stoning of Stephen relates to us as believers today. Going back to the beginning of this chapter for some background, Stephen is addressing the high priest, and the council. He begins to speak going back to Abraham giving their history, through him, on to Isaac, the covenant of circumcision, then onto Jacob, then the twelve patriarchs. Next he speaks of Joseph, his life in bondage in Egypt, God's being with him, delivering Joseph and giving him favor and wisdom in the sight of Pharaoh. Then he speaks of a famine in the land ultimately reuniting him with his family. After this Stephen speaks of Moses and the events of his life all the way to the time when God appeared to him in the burning bush on mount Sinai, saying, I am the God of thy fathers, the God of Abraham, and the God of Isaac, and the God of Jacob. Stephen goes on to speak of how God sent Moses to deliver his people out of bondage in Egypt, their time in the wilderness, their rebellion toward God, which ended with their being led captive into Babylon. Then Stephen speaks of David, and his desire to build a house for God, which was not granted to him, but instead to his son Solomon. All throughout his speaking to this council, he tells of God's presence and their rebellion and His deliverance. Stephen addresses them as stiffnecked and uncircumcised in heart and ears, always resisting the Holy Spirit. He says their fathers killed the prophets, who foretold the coming of Jesus, and how they had murdered Him. Then in verse 54 after hearing what Stephen had said, they became so furious that they gnashed on him with their teeth. But Stephen remained steadfast, full of the Holy Spirit, looked up into heaven and saw the glory of God and Jesus standing on His right hand. After this they cried out loudly, stopping their ears, ran upon him, seized him and stoned him in the presence of witnesses, one of whom was

Saul, later to become known as Paul. As they stoned Stephen, he was calling upon God, saying Lord Jesus, receive my spirit. He then knelt down and cried with a loud voice, asking God to not charge them with this sin. Then it says he fell asleep. You might be asking how this relates to us as believers today. With the events in our country and the world today, the way christians are being treated, many being persecuted, some losing their lives because of their faith, we do not know what we may face because of our faith. We may be like Stephen. We might have to face our enemies, our accusers, and suffer persecution or even death, which is not so far fetched as it may seem, due to the rapidly changing situations in our world. These things are happening today as we read this. There are those who hate us and want the Christian faith destroyed. If we are called to face this in our lifetime, I pray we may be like Stephen, holding steadfast, full of the Holy Spirit, looking up to heaven, to God and the Lord Jesus. I pray we may have the privilege of seeing as Stephen did, but if not, may we see through the eyes of our faith. And God forbid that we be called to give the ultimate sacrifice, like Stephen. But if that be so, may we, too, be able to ask the Lord to lay not the sins against us upon our enemies, remembering the words of Jesus to both love and forgive our enemies. And may God's Holy Spirit give us boldness and courage to face anything we are called to face, always looking unto Him!!!

Alleluia!!!

Laura Simpson   9-9-15

Thought for Today

2 Samuel 22:1-51

This is David's Song of Deliverance from all his enemies and from the hand of Saul. Do read the entire chapter. It is beautiful! I'm going to focus on verses 7-20. David speaks: In my distress I called upon the Lord, and cried to my God: and He did hear my voice out of His temple, and my cry did enter into His ears. Then the earth shook and trembled; the foundations of heaven moved and shook, because He was wroth. There went up a smoke out of His nostrils, and fire out of His mouth devoured: coals were kindled by it. He bowed the heavens also, and came down; and darkness was under His feet. And He rode upon a cherub, and did fly: and He was seen upon the wings of the wind. And He made darkness pavilions round about

59

Him, dark waters, and thick clouds of the skies. Through the brightness before Him were coals of fire kindled. The Lord thundered from heaven, and the most High uttered His voice. And He sent out arrows, and scattered them; lightning, and discomfited them. And the channels of the sea appeared, the foundations of the world were discovered, at the rebuking of the Lord, at the blast of the breath of His nostrils. He sent from above, He took me; He drew me out of many waters; He delivered me from my strong enemy, and from them that hated me: for they were too strong for me. They prevented me in the day of my calamity: but the Lord was my stay. He brought me forth also into a large place: He delivered me, because He delighted in me.

Comment: These are David's own words as he describes Almighty God while he watches His own deliverance. His words are awesome! His description of God as He moves is truly incredible! Read them and be blessed! Watch God at work as

He delivers one He loves dearly from his enemies! Then place yourself in David's position. Stop and realize He will do and does the very same for you and for me! Deliverance did not end with the Old Testament. He is God the Deliverer from the Beginning to the End! Look forward into the New Testament to the many times Jesus delivered those in need. David did not have to do anything, just stand back and watch God move on his behalf. The same is true for us, no matter what our need for deliverance may be. There are bondages of many kinds. Like David we cannot win these battles on our own. God calls us to stand back and watch Him work on our behalf! To trust Him as One who is willing and definitely able! Read 2 Chronicles 20:17 for more confirmation.

Alleluia!!!

Laura Simpson   9-4-15

Thought for Today

Yesterday I posted 2 Samuel: 22:1-51, focusing on verses 7-20. In these verses David describes watching Almighty God as He delivers David from his enemies and from Saul. Go back and read these verses if you have not. They are truly awesome! Today I want to focus on David's words to God and about God. Don't just read the words, hear them as he speaks! In verse 2 he said, The Lord is my rock, my fortress, and my deliverer; verse 3 The God of my rock; in Him will I trust: He is my shield, and the horn of my salvation, my high tower, and my refuge, my savior; Thou saves me from violence. Verse 4 says I will call on the Lord, who is worthy to be praised: so shall I be saved from mine enemies. In verses 5&6 David says he is compassed about by the waves of death and floods of ungodly men. He says he was afraid. Then in verse

7 David cries out to God. And just look at what Almighty God does! On to verse 20 David has been dramatically delivered by God, whom he says delights in him. In verses 21-25 David reveals his true love for God and his faithfulness to God and his commitment to live a life that is pleasing to God. He declares himself as righteous, his hands clean. He goes on to say that he has kept God's ways, not departing from them. Also has he kept God's judgments and statutes. In verse 24 David says he is free from sin and thus upright before God. Then in verse 25 he states that for these reasons God has recompensed him. The rest of the chapter is a multitude of praises to God from David. Verse 26 with the merciful Thou wilt show mercy. With the upright man Thou wilt show Thyself upright. Verse 27 With the pure Thou wilt show Thyself pure. Verse 28 the afflicted people Thou wilt save. Verse 29 Thou art my lamp, Thou wilt lighten my darkness. Verse 33 God is my strength and power, He maketh my way perfect. Verse 37 Thou has enlarged my steps so that my feet did

not slip. Verse 40 Thou hast girded me with strength to battle, Thou hast subdued under me those who rose up against me. Verse 44 Thou hast delivered me from the strivings of my people, Thou hast kept me to be the head of the heathen. Verse 47 The Lord liveth and blessed be my rock; and exalted be the God of the rock of my salvation. Verse 48 It is God that avengeth me. Verse 49 Thou hast delivered me from the violent man. In verse 50 David closes with praises to God and thanks, among the heathen. Lastly in verse 51 David declares God as his tower of salvation and a God who has showed him mercy and also to his seed. All through these words not one time does David take any credit, or draw any attention to himself. All his words give God the glory, praise and credit for his awesome deliverance and thanks for all God has done throughout his life. At the end David sees into the future. He sees God's hand upon his seed. And, as we know, now God has continued His work through David's seed to bring us our Messiah, the Lord Jesus Christ!!! How awesome is that!!!

Alleluia!!!

Laura Simpson   9-5-15

More Thoughts for Today

As I sit here this afternoon reflecting on the passage from 2 Samuel 22:1-51, my thoughts are toward a connection between David and the church today in our nation. When I say the church, I am referring to the true church, not those people who go to a building on Sunday and call it worship. I am talking about those people who make up the Bride of Christ. Those who love God, those who have given their hearts and lives to the Lord Jesus Christ, those who walk in the power of His Holy Spirit. Those people who will be ushered into heaven, and not told by the Lord Jesus Christ, you are one of many who called Me, Lord, Lord, but will not enter in. In 2 Samuel 22 it is stated that David was ruler of a heathen nation. He was relentlessly pursued by his enemies, and he was much afraid. He acknowledged God as

Lord. He knew that God was his deliverer. He called on God to help him. Then God allowed David to watch as He delivered him. An awesome account! He then says that God rewarded him because of his righteousness, cleanliness, uprightness, and obedience. Lastly, David speaks a multitude of words praising God, and telling who God is, what is His character. Now fast forward to the true church today. Like David we have for many, many years been the leader in our nation. But not so now. We are now surrounded by enemies, also called heathens, who seek to destroy us. And they, too, are relentless in their pursuits. Like David I must admit that I am afraid at times. We as His people acknowledge Him as God. And I believe we would all agree that the church and our nation can be delivered by God, certainly not our government. Vitally important here is we must act now and call on God to deliverer us, just as David did in his day. Wouldn't it be awesome if God would allow us, like David, to watch as He delivers us? There's just one block. Unlike David, we the true church, are not clean. Our leaders have let down teaching the seriousness of sin in God's eyes. We have come to treat it casually, much of the time excusing our sins, and at times giving our sins another label. And so many neglect reading God's Word thus being ignorant of what He says about sin. Here's what God's answer is for the Church and our nation. 2Chronicles 7:14 if My people, which are called by My name, shall humble themselves, and pray, and seek My face, and turn from their wicked ways; then will I hear from heaven, and will forgive their sin, and will heal their land. Please note here that God calls His people to obey this word from Him, not the heathen in the land! But also in obeying His command, because of His Church/His people, our land will be healed!!! Body of Christ, let's get on our knees, confess our sins, call on the only One who can deliver us, praying for our church and our nation and watch our God as He delivers us all!!! Remember again, His Words do not return void!!! We will then have a praise gathering, like none other, thanking Him for His mercy and love, His forgiveness and restoration!!!

All Glory be unto Him alone!!!

Alleluia!!!

Laura Russell Simpson

Thought For Today

O, For A Thousand Tongues To Sing
My Great Redeemers Praise!!!

Let's join together this day as we worship Him and sing from within our hearts with the same depth from which these words come!!!

Alleluia!!!

Laura Simpson   12-27-15

Happy Sabbath!!!

Thought for Today

Psalm 90:14. O satisfy us early with Thy mercy; that we may rejoice and be glad all our days.

Comment: I discovered this verse years ago. It is so beautiful to me. Over the years I have prayed it over my daughter and then my grandson. My prayer was, according to this verse, for God to bring my children to Him at early ages, so that they would rejoice over His goodness, rejoice over their salvation, and experience gladness in their hearts and lives as they walk with Him all their lives. Verse 12 before this speaks of teaching us to number our days, so that we may apply our hearts unto wisdom. This again, I pray for not only myself, but my children. Wouldn't it be wonderful for our children to learn this, also, and to learn it early in their lives? Lastly, verse15 asks

God to make us glad according to the days wherein He hast afflicted us. As we walk this out in our lives, it is hard. However, I'm sure we would all agree, after we have come through afflictions, we have gladness in our hearts. Gladness for an increase in our faith, gladness for God's presence with us during these times, gladness for His help and comfort, gladness that He does see us through hard times, and gladness for what He has taught us in these times of affliction. Again, I pray this for my children. I'm sure you agree that we all want these for each of our children. The earlier our children come to know Him, the easier it will be for them to handle what life has for them. To have Him on their journey is my heart's desire. And the earlier, the better. In closing, I hope these verses will inspire each of you, as you pray for those who are so precious to you and to Him! And for ourselves, also. Alleluia!!!

Laura Simpson   8-29-15

Share a Thought for Today

Psalm 51:12. Restore unto me the joy of Thy salvation; and uphold me with Thy free spirit.

Just sitting on my porch reflecting on the events of this week, which is quickly coming to a close, my thoughts are on the goodness of God. I am so very thankful for the joy He has given to me. These thoughts brought me to this scripture. It has been a long journey, and oftentimes a difficult one, very difficult at times, which has brought me to this place. For the first time in my life I know what the unspeakable joy is that He gives us. Read 1 Peter 1:8. And it only comes from Him. I cannot tell you how much fun I have had writing the Share a Laughs! Life's ordinary events can truly be hilarious! You cannot imagine how much I have laughed as these thoughts rolled onto my page! But in case any of you would think that my life is nothing but laughter and fun, I want each of you to know that I still have struggles, problems, and days with shedding tears. There are days I lose my joy, just like David wrote about in this verse. But with God's grace, if I get my focus back on Him instead of my issues, then He restores my joy. I have learned, too, that when struggles come, if I keep my eyes on Him, I can still have that unspeakable joy. And I have learned that any sin will cause me to lose my joy. I try to make that right at once. David calls it the joy of Thy salvation! And indeed it is just that! Notice he does not say my salvation, instead, Thy salvation. This brings to mind the journey we begin with Him at our salvation. Joy unspeakable is only one of the multitude of things He offers us as we walk in His Spirit. It's there for us. We just need to receive it. Sometimes, I believe we through ignorance of His Words, deprive ourselves of experiencing Him and who He really is. In closing, if anyone reading this has lost your joy or maybe never had it, I urge you to pray like David and ask God to restore the joy of His salvation to you. Through faith in Him I believe He will answer your prayer. We must remember that He desires to see us live in victory, not defeat. Do we not want the same for our children? Why would He not answer that prayer? He has for me and He will for you, also. That's just who He is!

P.S. This week I experienced one of the hardest days I have ever had. But at the same time I have never had a week where I laughed so much. For a brief moment my joy was seemingly lost, but when I refocused my thoughts toward Him, it returned very soon. I sincerely pray this prayer for each of you. May each of you reading this message have His joy unspeakable!

Alleluia!!!

Laura Simpson   8-28-15

Satan is alive and well. Believe it? You better. I just walked face forward into another one of his attacks. But just to set him straight from the beginning, this lesson is not to give him any credit, pleasure, or importance. He is a defeated foe. We just need to tell him just that. And that I do at this very moment! From there I would like to share with you what God has taught me about the enemy of our souls. Our Lord wants us to recognize how Satan operates. John 10:10 tells us the thief comes to steal, kill, and destroy. He will steal whatever he can from us, our peace, our joy, among other things. Just in case you don't think he attacks our bodies seeking to kill us just look at Job. In Job 1 Satan talks to God twice seeking to destroy Job. God allows him anything but Job's life. The first thing Satan does is attack Job physically with boils. On a very personal level for two days I have been having high blood pressure. My sleep has been great, no anxiety, very peaceful. I have been applying God's Word, James 4:7, Resist the devil, and he will flee from you. Just one hour ago with prayer with my dear cousin, my top number went from 165 down to 111. Praise God! His Word does not return void, just like He says. (Isaiah 55:11) Back to our enemy, he comes to destroy us however he can make it work. He will destroy relationships, our faith in God, our witness for Christ, and on and on. Satan delights to control our thoughts. He will fire those darts of anger, envy, hate, jealousy, greed, lust, bitterness, and that list also goes on. He will lead us to feel we have no worth, our sins are too bad for God to forgive, and so on. But remember he is the "Father of Lies". (John 8:44) God's Word also warns us Satan roams around like a roaring lion seeking whom he may devour. (1 Peter 5:8) In this verse God tells us to be sober and vigilant. With God's help we will come to recognize these attacks as they come and also with God's help we can have complete victory over our enemy. Believing God's Word, and applying it will give us the victory. From this we see how God warns us and informs us as we encounter the enemy. But He also shows us how to protect ourselves from Satan. He tells us there is an armor we have, His armor, to put on. (Ephesians 6:11&13) It is complete from head to toe. He tells us our shield is our faith, and our sword of His Spirit is the Word of God. Also we have the helmet of hope (1 Thessalonians 5:8), the hope of salvation, and the breastplate of faith and love. He tells us again in this verse to be sober. Powerful words, aren't they? Indeed He covers it all. Must I say how important it is to know our Lord and know His Word? If we are not informed of the tactics of our enemy, and do not know how to fight him, he will truly devour us one step at a time. Remember, too, we will not be tempted above what we are able to bear, but God will make a way of escape (1 Corinthians 10:13). Isn't He so good to us? He truly wants us to live a victorious life with Him. I want to add one more thing. Satan can only take what we give him. So I say let's starve that devouring lion with the knowledge and protection of the God whose Spirit lives in His very own children.

Alleluia!!!

Laura Simpson   8-7-15

Well Friends, the enemy has struck again. I look at God's Words again. First thing I see is He's offering me more grace if I humble myself. Then I submit myself to Him, resist the devil and watch him flee. Next I draw near to my Father, and feel His presence as He comes to help me. Thank you, Lord, that you know I need your help right now. But I must be clean, also. My reaction right now is not godly. So, I confess. I have a choice to make right now. I can either act or react. If I react my choice will be in the flesh. I'm not going that route. So I choose to act on the promises I just read. You can take it and go, Satan. I will not give you the credit, pleasure, or power of thinking you have any hold on me. I choose to tell you that I will not let you ruin what's left of a beautiful day. In spite of your attack, I will turn my thoughts to things that are pure, lovely, holy, and of good report. In fact, I'm feeling better already!!!

Laura Simpson   8-22-15

One thing more. Thanks, friends, for allowing me to express my feelings to you all. I have just come to realize that it expends too much energy to hold on to hard feelings, etc. At my age I need to protect all the energy I have! And above that, I want to live happily ever after!!!

Looks like Satan is working overtime today. He sure hit me hard. Let me share what God taught me recently about confronting Satan. I am learning to have victory over him as I apply these scriptures. Look at James 4:6-8. But He giveth more grace. Wherefore He saith, God resisteth the proud, but giveth grace unto the humble. Submit yourselves therefore to God. Resist the devil, and he will flee from you. Draw nigh to God, and He will draw nigh to you. Cleanse your hands, ye sinners; and purify your hearts, ye double minded. I believe we can have victory over Satan by obeying these words from God. He first offers us more grace as we humble ourselves. We must confess any pride we have in any area of our lives, thinking we can do it on our own. We need His help. So we must confess and humble ourselves before Him. We need His help to have victory over Satan's attacks. This is when His grace comes. Then He tells us to submit ourselves to Him. Next He says to resist the devil, and he will flee. Remember here that His Word does not return void. This is a promise from Him. After that, He says to draw nigh to Him, and He will draw nigh to us. Lastly He tells us we must be clean in our hands and hearts. He is addressing the double minded. We can't be both. Our minds must be on Him. We need His forgiveness. As we obey these words, I believe He will help us have victory over the enemy of our souls. I have been applying these words when I come under attack, and I am seeing victory as He helps me. Satan is relentless, but greater is He that is in us than he that is in the world!

Alleluia!!!

Laura Simpson   8-21-15

More Thoughts For Today

The race is on. Let's put our faith in 4 wheel drive and leave Satan behind choking on our dust! The checkered flag has already come down. We are already declared the winners. The only thing left is to cross the finish line and receive our prize!!! And what a prize it will be!!! And Satan will be making his last "pit stop"!!! Hallelujah!!!

Laura Simpson   11-21-15

My prayer for Today

Phil4:6&7. Be anxious for nothing, but in everything by prayer and supplication, with thanksgiving, let your requests be made known to God and the peace of God, which surpasses all understanding, will guard your hearts and minds through Christ Jesus.

First of all, Lord, I give You this day. Help me to walk in Your Spirit, not the flesh. It is the flesh that causes anxieties and stress. You show us the path from anxiety to Your peace in this verse. It is through prayer with thanksgiving that You tell us to give our needs to You. I give You thanks for all Your goodness to me, thanks from Your Word for Your desire to see us stress free, and without worry. Thank You that right now I give you my requests for today, requests for You to slow me down. I ask

You to help me walk this day one step at a time, not being overwhelmed, looking at all the events of my day at one time. Most important of all is my desire to keep my focus on You. In obedience to Your Word, Your promise is Your peace, which will guard my heart and my mind in Christ Jesus. What an awesome promise! You are guarding my mind when it goes on overload, and guarding my heart when the enemy of my soul seeks to destroy what Your Holy Spirit has accomplished in me. He seeks to destroy the fruit of Your Spirit that He has so graciously produced in me, one step at a time. I ask You to show me this day when I step out of Your Spirit. Bring my thoughts back to You. I thank You for the victory I will have as I walk in obedience to Your Word! And in the power of Your very own Spirit!

Alleluia!!!

Laura Simpson 8-20-15

As of this writing Bill and I are waiting to hear whether or not he will need open heart surgery, and if so, when. You might think that I am anxious and worried. But not so. I want to share what God has told me about waiting on Him. Isaiah 40:31 says, But those who wait on the Lord shall renew their strength; they shall mount up with wings like eagles, they shall run and not be weary, they shall walk and not faint. Job 14:14-16 says, If a man dies, shall he live again? All the days of my hard service I will wait, till my change comes. You shall call, and I will answer you; you shall desire the work of your hands, for now you number my steps,... Lamentations 3:25-32 says, the Lord is good to those who wait for Him, to the soul who seeks Him. It is good that one should hope and wait quietly for the salvation of the Lord. It is good for a man to bear the yoke in his youth. Let him sit alone and keep silent, because God has laid it on him; let him put his mouth in the dust-there may yet be hope. Let him give his cheek to the one who strikes him, and be full of reproach. For the Lord will not cast off forever. Though He causes grief, yet He will show compassion according to the multitude of His mercies. Verse 38 says, Is it not from the mouth of the Most High that woe and well-being proceed? In Isaiah 40:31 Isaiah speaks of those who wait on the Lord. I ask, "wait for what?" What I hear in waiting is giving God time to work out His purposes in our lives. Remember He orders our steps and fashions our days. During our times of waiting, we can rest knowing that a time will come when His purposes are accomplished. Also as we wait, we must trust. Then look what He offers us-- a renewed strength, the strength of eagle wings. We can run and not be weary and walk and not faint all because we have had a time of rest while we waited. Going back to Psalm 40 David said he waited patiently for the Lord. He goes on to reveal this as a time of prayer. In these verses I hear that David was not striving, but resting and praying. Just look at what God was doing in David's life during this time. Do go back and read Psalm 40 again. It, too, speaks to us of a time when God was hard at work, working out His purposes and ultimately bringing David to an awesome place where He would use him greatly. In Job 14:14-16 we see the same principals. Job is in a hard place, a time of affliction; but he, too, says, I will wait till my change comes. Can't you just hear his patience and trust in the Lord? He, too, reveals it as a time of prayer; and he also sees how God is ordering his steps as he waits. Job's faith shines through these passages. Then in Lamentations 3:25-32, Jeremiah, who is believed to be the author of this book, speaks of how good God is to those who wait for Him. I see in this how the Lord rewards our faith and trust in Him as we, too, cease our striving and give Him time to work His purposes in our lives. Verse 26 calls us to wait quietly for His help. Jeremiah adds how good it is for us during these times of affliction. He says, sit alone and keep silent. He says no complaining or blaming. God is at work. Verse 31 tells us that these times are not forever. And lastly in verse 32, even though God allows these times, as Jeremiah puts it, times of grief, yet our Father will show compassion, revealing to us the multitude of His mercies. So once again we see in these passages a call to wait on the Lord in patience, rest, quietness, and trust. Also these are times we are called to prayer as we allow our God time to work in our lives as He brings us out rested and strong to that wonderful place that only He can achieve. Just look at the final awesome result. It is a place where He will use us to touch others (Psalm 40:3).

Alleluia!!!

Laura Simpson   8-8-15

Do you feel like you're in a pit? Are you going through a time of suffering? Maybe you feel hopeless. Well, I've got good news. Oh, and maybe you wonder how I know. Well, I've been there and been there more than once. I speak through my own experiences. I testify first of all that God is with you, and He does not waste any of our sufferings. As a matter of fact, He uses them to grow us and above all to bring Him the glory. In order to show us how He works in our pits and prisons, whatever you want to label yours, He gives us the person and life of Joseph. Read beginning in Genesis 37 through chapter 50. It is awesome what He shows us in these chapters which speak directly to those of us who might be trying to dig out of a pit or prison. First of all Joseph was thrown into a literal pit by his own family who hated him. Then they sold him to a group of Midianite traders who took Joseph to Egypt. As God would have it, he was bought by Potiphar, an officer of Pharaoh, captain of the guard also an Egyptian. Genesis 39:2 says, The Lord was with Joseph, and he was a successful man; and he was in the house of his master the Egyptian. Verse 3 says, And his master saw that the Lord was with him and that the Lord made all he did to prosper in his hand. Verse 4 says, so Joseph found favor in his sight. In verse 5 it says that the Lord blessed the Egyptian's house for Joseph's sake. From these verses we see God with Joseph. We see him taken to a place that does not worship the God he serves, and then we see Joseph used as a witness to God's power in his life. The Egyptian or non-believer is then blessed because of the believer (Joseph). Next he is accused of raping his master's wife which is a lie against Joseph. So consequently, he is thrown into prison. Genesis 39:21 says, But the Lord was with Joseph and showed him mercy, and He gave him favor in the sight of the keeper of the prison. All the prisoners were put under his charge. So now Joseph finds himself in prison because of a lie, but God is still with him and still showing him favor. While in prison God uses Joseph to interpret the dreams of the king's butler and baker who have been imprisoned also. Joseph also is called to interpret the dream of Pharaoh. Notice chapter 41:16. Joseph answered Pharaoh saying, It is not in me. God will give Pharaoh an answer of peace. So we see while in prison, God is using Joseph; but Joseph does not take any credit. He gives God the glory. Remember, all this pit and prison stuff started at the age of seventeen. Joseph is now thirty years old. So he has been in this place for a long time. God didn't seem to be in any hurry to bring Joseph out. Next, Joseph is made second in command only to the king. He was set over all the land of Egypt. A famine came in all lands except Egypt. It says in Egypt there was bread. In his God-given wisdom Joseph had prepared the country for this famine. As a result all countries came to Joseph to buy grain. It was for this reason that Joseph's family came to Egypt for food, not knowing that he was even still alive. After a time with his brothers, Joseph identifies himself and says to them, But now, do not be grieved or angry with yourselves because you sold me here. For God sent me before you to preserve life. (Chapter 45:5) Verse 8 says, So now it was not you who sent me here, but God. In these verses God uses Joseph to save his family. He takes all the blame and guilt off of his family and again gives God the glory. Joseph acknowledges that this was all in God's plan. In closing can you see yourself in any or all of this? Know that in our pits, prisons, and sufferings, God is with us, and He has a plan for us. During these times He uses us and helps us. Joseph never blamed God, but always gave God the glory. And so should we. And he never blamed others for all the suffering he went through. Joseph also showed no bitterness for his circumstances. And again so should we. God has given Joseph to us as a awesome example for us to follow. No matter how deep the pit there is a plan in it, and hopefully, like Joseph's, ours will be used by God to reach many people and as Joseph stated to preserve lives. Alleluia!!!

Laura Simpson   4-28-15

Psalm 40

I waited patiently for the Lord;
And He inclined to me,
And heard my cry.
He also brought me up out of a horrible pit,
Out of the miry clay,
And set my feet upon a rock,
And established my steps.
He has put a new song in my mouth –
Praise to our God;
Many will see it and fear,
And will trust in the Lord.

Preface

This message is not a devotional. It is a study, a continuation on the life and example of Joseph. It may seem long and repetitious. That's because it is. However, the reason it is, is to see how many, many times the scriptures reveal these subjects. Read it slowly and prayerfully. If you need a break, read the message and then come back later and read the scriptures and closing. If you are not seeking a closer relationship with God, this study is not for you.

As you read this message today I pray you will see the mercy, goodness, and grace of God and also His faithfulness to His children. May His name be glorified as we look into His Word and hear what He says about affliction and "the appointed time". Once again His message begins with the life and example of Joseph. This time it comes not from Genesis, but from Psalm 105. It begins in verse 16. It says, Moreover He called for a famine in the land; He destroyed all the provision of bread. Verse 17 - He sent a man before them - Joseph - who was sold as a slave. Verse 18 - They hurt his feet with fetters, He was laid in irons. Verse 19 - Until the time that His word came to pass, the Word of the Lord tested him. Verse 20 - The king sent and released him, the ruler of the people let him go free. Verse 21 - He made him lord of his house, and ruler of all his possessions, Verse 22 - To bind his princes at his pleasure, And teach his elders wisdom. If you have not read the message I wrote earlier on the life and example of Joseph, taken from Genesis, I urge you to read it first. This message today is a continuation of that one, focusing on affliction and the appointed time. Joseph suffered many afflictions. And I say, too, that his afflictions lasted many years. In the Genesis account it states that God was always with him. And Joseph always gave God the glory. Then, too, God used Joseph greatly to work out His purpose. After Joseph had served his purpose, God brought him out – at the appointed time. Back to Psalm 105. Verse 19 says, Until the time that His word came to pass, The Word of the Lord tested him. There is another Psalm which speaks of affliction and purpose and the appointed time. Psalm 40 says, I waited patiently for the Lord; And He inclined to me, And heard my cry. He also brought me up out of a horrible pit, out of the miry clay, and set my feet upon a rock, and established my steps. He has put a new song in my mouth - Praise to our God; Many will see it and fear, And will trust in the Lord. I call Psalm 40 the Song of Joseph. We, too, experience afflictions throughout our lives. Sometimes ours, like Joseph's, last a long time. But God is there with us, too, working out His purpose. And at God's appointed time, He will bring us out. Like Psalm 40 says, He will put a new song in our mouth – Praise to our God. And lastly, He will use our afflictions. Hopefully, our experiences in the pits and prisons will become a testimony for others to see it and fear, and will trust in the Lord. Like Joseph, our sufferings are never wasted. In the end God used Joseph to save many people. But it all happened in His appointed time.

Alleluia!!!

Laura Simpson   5-30-15

* For further study, see following pages

The Appointed Time

Psalm 105:19 Until the time that His Word came to pass, the Word of the Lord tested him (Joseph).

Gen 18:14 Is anything too hard for the Lord? At the appointed time I will return to you, according to the time of life, and Sarah shall have a son.

Ex. 9:5 Then the Lord appointed a set time saying, Tomorrow the Lord will do this thing in the land.

Num 9:2 Let the children of Israel keep the Passover at its appointed time.

Job 7:1 Is there not a time of hard service for man on earth?

Psalm 104:19 He appointed the moon for seasons; the sun knows its going down.

Dan. 8:19 And He said, Look, I am making known to you what shall happen in the latter time of the indignation; for at the appointed time the end shall be.

Dan 11:27 Both these kings' hearts shall be bent on evil, and they shall speak lies at the same table; but it shall not prosper, for the end will still be at the appointed time.

Acts 17:31 Because He has appointed a day on which He will judge the world in righteousness by the Man whom He has ordained.

Heb. 9:27 And as it is appointed for men to die once, but after this the judgment.

Mark 13:24-27 But in those days, after that tribulation, the sun will be darkened, and the moon will not give its light; the stars of heaven will fall, and the powers in heaven will be shaken. Then they will see the Son of Man coming in the clouds with great power and glory. And then He will send His angels, and gather together His elect from the four winds, from the farthest part of earth to the farthest part of heaven.

Affliction

Nahum 1:12 Though I have afflicted you, I will afflict you no more. For now I will break off his yoke from you, and burst your bonds apart.

Gen. 15:13 Then He said to Abram. Know certainly that your descendants will be strangers in a land that is not theirs, and will serve them, and they will afflict them four hundred years.

Lam. 3:31&32 For the Lord will not cast off forever. Though He causes grief, yet He will show compassion according to the multitude of His mercies.

Lam. 3:22 Through the Lord's mercies we are not consumed, because His compassions fail not.

Psalm 119:67 Before I was afflicted I went astray. But now I keep your word.

Psalm 119:71 It is good for me that I have been afflicted that I may learn Your statutes.

Strong's Concordance is full of scriptures on the appointed time and afflictions. I have listed only a few. In each and all of them you hear not only how we all go through afflictions and how God brings us through. We also hear purpose.

Psalm 37:23&24 says, The steps of a good man are ordered by the Lord, and He delights in his way. Though he fall, he shall not be utterly cast down; for the Lord upholds him with His hand.

Can you hear in this verse the steps of affliction, the steps of "appointed times", and the steps of purpose?

Psalm 139:16 Your eyes saw my substance, being yet unformed. And in Your book they all were written, the days fashioned for me, when as yet there were none of them.

I believe the days fashioned for me means the days fashioned for afflictions, the days fashioned for purposes, and the days fashioned for "the appointed times" before our last appointed time.

Alleluia and Amen

Let Psalm 40 be your song, too!
I thank God it is mine!!!

Got a prayer need? Something you have really been praying about for a long time? Are you getting discouraged? Feel like God isn't listening? It's been a long time and you're not seeing any answers. You are standing on the promises of God as given in His Word. You might be saying, Lord, You say we have not because we ask not. And, Lord, I am asking. Your faith says I believe You hear and answer. He says when you pray, pray believing you will receive and you will. You don't doubt because you know He is able. You pray in the name of Jesus, just like He tells you to do. You have confessed your sins so that no sin will block your prayers. You know that His word does not return void. Still no answer? In the meantime Satan is hitting you hard. He is whispering thoughts of doubt and more discouragement in your ear. Well, just now God speaks. And this is what He says, Having done all to stand. Dig your feet in kind of stand . Before you dig your feet in He gives you some help. That is to put on His armor so that you can fight off all those fiery darts Satan is throwing at you. Put on the helmet of salvation which guards your mind. Next the breastplate of righteousness which guards your heart. Then the girdle of truth around your waist. After that the gospel of peace on your feet. And above all take up the shield of faith and the sword of the Spirit which is the Word of God. We know already that the Word is our weapon. It is on the Word that our prayers hinge. So after we put on His armor, we don't do anything more – We just stand. The next move is up to Him. And He will move. He reminds us that as we call on Him, He will show us great and mighty things which we know not. (Jeremiah 33:3) As we stand we just have to trust, and at "the appointed time" the answer will come. Remember, the effective, fervent prayer of a righteous man avails much. (James 5:16)

Alleluia!!!

Laura Simpson   4-23-15

Matthew 4:4 But He (Jesus) answered and said, It is written, Man shall not live by bread alone, but by every Word that proceeds from the mouth of God.

First look at whom Jesus was answering. His enemy, Satan, had just started to tempt Him. I want to note here that they were in the wilderness. Jesus overcame the temptation by quoting the Word of God. He started each reply to Satan's three temptations with "It is written", and then He quoted the three scriptures. He overcame each time. Jesus set the example for us. He tells us we are to live by every Word that proceeds from the mouth of God. What a statement! God is trying to tell us how very important His Word is. If we don't know the Word, we have no defense against Satan; and he is our enemy, too. We simply have to read His Word, or we will be overcome by what God tells us we are fighting against. Ephesians 6:12 tells us, For we do not wrestle against flesh and blood, but against principalities, against powers, against the rulers of the darkness of this age, against spiritual hosts of wickedness in the heavenly places. Scary, isn't it? Makes me want to go get my Bible and start reading. How about you? But God doesn't leave us defenseless. He tells us (Ephesians 6:10-17) to put on His armor and to take up the shield of faith and the sword of the Spirit, which is the Word of God. He also says in Hebrews 4:12, For the Word of God is living and powerful, and sharper than any two-edged sword. Here again the Word is our weapon against the temptations Satan throws at us. God calls them the wiles of the devil. (Hebrews 6:11) No matter what the temptation is, we, too, if we know the Word, can reply with "It is written" and then quote a scripture. If it is fear, anxiety, worry, envy, strife, selfishness, greed, hate, lust and the list goes on; we are given the weapon to overcome. And when we succumb, so many times, like Jesus, we, too, are in a wilderness place. It's a choice we make. God does not force Himself on us. He does not force us to read His Word, but look at the alternative. The alternative is a life of defeat. Let's choose to live a life of victory by reading our Bibles each day and overcoming by the Word of God. Alleluia!!!

Laura Simpson   4-18-15

Thought for Today

Mark 4:35-41

On the same day, when evening had come, He said to them, let us cross over to the other side. Now when they had left the multitude, they took Him along in the boat as He was. And other little boats were also with Him. And a great windstorm arose, and the waves beat into the boat, so that it was already filling. But He was in the stern, asleep on a pillow. And they awoke Him and said to Him, Teacher, do You not care that we are perishing? Then He arose and rebuked the wind, and said to the sea, Peace, be still! And the wind ceased and there was a great calm. But He said to them, Why are you so fearful? How is it that you have no faith? And they feared exceedingly, and said to one another, who can this be, that even the wind and the sea obey Him?

Peace Be Still! Just reading these words gives me a good feeling, a feeling of comfort in my soul, and a recognizing that my Lord, the Prince of Peace, is present and speaking to me. I feel myself not needing to be in control. That is in the hands of one greater than I. Can you just hear Him as He speaks the peace He says is the peace I leave with you? I feel myself relax just now. Do you and I, like those in the boat, have an angry storm raging? Are our boats filling up? Are You sure You're awake, Lord Jesus? Help Lord, I'm sinking. Lord, are You sure You care? I'm scared, Lord. My faith is being tested. And oh, my Lord, thank You that You didn't rebuke me. You rebuked the storm instead. You commanded the storm with, Peace be Still! However, You did ask me why I was so afraid and what about my faith. You have taught me a big lesson for the storms, which will come. The One whom even the wind and sea obey is the One who is in command of my angry storms. You say again, Peace Be Still! My fears, my need to control, and my lack of faith subside as I hear Your words. And then there is a great calm.

Alleluia!!!

Laura Simpson   4-16-15

Listen as we hear what God says about His Word. In Isaiah 56:11 He says, So shall My Word be that goes forth from My mouth; it shall not return to Me void, but it shall accomplish what I please. And it shall prosper in the thing for which I sent it. Just think of all the many promises He has spoken to us. They are straight from the mouth of Almighty God. They are not empty promises. His Word accomplishes something in us, whatever that promise may be. And even in us He prospers His Word. Oh, Father, how good You are to us. Thank You for your precious Word! Thank You for the Words You give us to live by, promises to help us through tough times, promises to let us know You are always with us, promises that tell us You not only hear our prayers but answer them when we ask believing and in Jesus' name. And there are so many more, a Bible full of them. When we read Your Word, help us not to read it casually, but to hear Your voice as You speak to us through it. Let us give thanks to You as we can know that You are a God of Your Word. You do what You say.

Hebrews 13:5 I will never leave you or forsake you. He means just that. He will never leave you.

Psalm 46:1 God is our refuge and strength. A very present help in trouble. Therefore we will not fear. And He means just that. He will help us.

Jeremiah 33:3 Call to Me, and I will answer you, and show you great and mighty things, which you do not know. Oh, Father, what a promise!!!

Lord God, May Your Word prosper in us as we through faith believe it and receive it unto ourselves. Amen and Alleluia!!!

Folks, we've got to read the Word if we want to live the abundant life He wants to give us.

Laura Simpson   4-12-15

Father, You said, Be still and know that I
am God. You also said, In quietness and
confidence shall be my strength. And
Jesus said, Peace, be still, when He calmed
the angry storm. I hear You calling us to a
place where we can meet You, away from
the clatter of the world which so distracts
us. In the stillness we meet the One who
is the I am God, that is the I AM, the I AM
God. How awesome! In the quietness with
You we come away strengthened. Because
You alone are trustworthy beyond doubt,
we can have divine confidence. And Jesus
offers us peace in the stillness, a peace like
no one else can give except Him. It comes
in the form of a command, and it runs
deep within our being. Tonight as I write,
I am still. It is quiet. Peace is present. I

have just spent time with the great I AM, and He spoke to me in His still small voice. Alleluia!!!

Laura Simpson   4-9-15

Thought For Today

Psalm 119:28 My soul melteth for heaviness: strengthen Thou me according unto Thy word.

For each of us our struggles are different. But one thing is certain. We all go through times of hardships. As this verse says, there are times when we are weighed down. Times when our souls are heavy from the load we carry. And many times our relief is a long time coming. Remember, God is not in a hurry. As we go through these times, He is working out His plan for us. And oftentimes, we hinder His progress. We try desperately to fix the problem ourselves. We hold onto it, struggling and striving, with our focus being on the circumstances, instead of Him. It truly is so much easier to give it to Him than to hold onto it. The writer of this verse in Psalm 119 knew where to go for strength. He went to the Word of God. And I will tell you at this point how important it is to know God's Word. If we do not know God's Word, we do not know our Father. We do not know His truths. We do not know His promises to each of us. Jesus, being the Living Word, literally walks off the pages of the Bible! He, through His Holy Spirit, reveals His Words to each of us personally. As we read the Word, apply the Word, stand on the Word, and speak forth the Word; we will soon recognize that this gives us strength. At this point I will encourage you to not just read His words, but hear His Words! As you read He will speak to you personally. Another word of encouragement, pray His Words back to Him. Talk to the King in the King's own language! You will make your Father smile, and I assure you, He will bless you greatly! The more of His Word you know, the greater your strength will become. Therefore, in times of weakness, meditate

Laura Russell Simpson

on His Words, and watch as He takes you from weakness to strength!!!

Alleluia!!!

Laura Simpson   1-1-16

Thought For Today

Psalm 84:7 They go from strength to strength.

Exodus 33:14 And He said, My presence shall go with thee, and I will give thee rest.

II Samuel 22:40 For Thou hast girded me with strength to battle. Yes, life is hard, sometimes very hard, and sometimes even brutal. We all go through times of hardship, times of suffering and pain, difficult times, and times when our Father will test our faith. He tells us in Psalm 84:7 that we go from strength to strength. But before this strength is manifested, we go from struggle to struggle. These times appear often in our own personal journeys. My prayer is that as you look back, you will recognize that through these times you were strengthened. Again I share with you that I would not be where I am today had it not been for the times of struggles and sufferings and difficulties. I am truly thankful for those times God took me from weakness to strength. Look at Exodus 33:14. He tells us, My presence goes with you. He says, also, He will never leave us or forsake us. So from struggle to struggle His presence is with us to give us strength. Even before we go into a time of struggle or hardship, He has already provided for us. II Samuel 22:40 says, For Thou hast girded me with strength to battle. It is there for us; however, we must go into the battle first. Then His strength will manifest itself. God knows our weaknesses. He knows we need His help. And He is telling us how very much He wants to help us. We are never left to ourselves, alone in our struggles! As already stated, His presence is there with us. And as also stated, He has prepared us for the battles we face by girding us with strength before we go into our battles. As we go from battle to battle, our weaknesses become our strengths! It is from these times that He increases our faith. When we grasp these truths we are not overcome when another battle comes. We must learn to look beyond our weaknesses/circumstances to what will come. And what we will see through our faith is strength. God will prove Himself each time, proving Himself faithful to His Word!!! So do not despair in your times of battle. Remember, My strength is made perfect in your weakness!!! And do not miss the end of the scripture. He will give us rest!!! Preparation for the next time we will struggle, and rest from what we have just been through. Again, He says to us, I know you need My help, and I want so badly to give you that help. Through these Words of His come His great love for each of us!!! Let's not miss our blessing!!!

Alleluia!!!

Laura Simpson   1-1-16

On June 2 at 9:15 that morning, my daughter and I left our home going to two appointments facing the possibility of having two kinds of cancer. I had symptoms of both. I left having no fear, no anxiety, only the peace that surpasses all understanding. The previous week-end I had spent with Him in prayer. I knew that no matter what the outcome, I was in His care. Once again only peace, no fear, no anxiety. Only God Himself knows how deeply I believe that He heals. His Word is full of scriptures on healing and scriptures which show us how He honors our faith. At this point I want to tell that I have already been healed of a stroke I had a little over one year ago, and at this time I am not diabetic, having been diagnosed several years ago. All glory belongs to Him. Now back to June 2. He had spoken to me a couple of weeks before through a scripture. It says, I have plans for you, plans to prosper you, to give you a hope and a future.

Jeremiah 29:11

All that day I kept hearing, "I have plans for you". As I sat in the waiting room at the Women's Diagnostic Center a conversation began. Several of the ladies, like me, had been called back for more mammograms because of abnormal findings on their last ones. The mood was solemn. One lady spoke up and told us that she had just come from having an MRI on her brain. She said she was falling and had been having headaches for three months. Now she was facing breast cancer possibly. With tears in her eyes she said, this has not been a good day. I spoke up at this point and said, "I would like to share a scripture with you." I looked at them and said, "God's

Word says, the steps of a good man are ordered by the Lord." (Psalm 37:23) Today our steps are ordered. Other ladies began to speak of their faith. Continuing on, I said that Jesus' death on the cross was for our salvation, but also for our healing. I shared the scripture which says, that by His stripes we are healed (I Peter 2:24). Yes, there is healing. God's Holy Spirit led me on to share the study of Joseph that I had just done. Through me, as I humbly give God the glory, He spoke to these ladies about affliction and suffering, about His presence through it all, about His purpose in it, and how as in the life of Joseph, God brought Him out at His appointed time. (Genesis chapters 37-45 & Psalm 105:16-22). I looked at them intently and said, "In the appointed time, God will bring us out." With that, I was called back for more views and an ultrasound. To each one in my path, praises to God came from my lips. At 1:00 p.m. I left there with a clear report. If there was any cancer present, He healed it. Going on to my gynecologist, having symptoms that cancer from 2009 might be returning, I had examinations and another ultrasound. During that time I once again, through the words of the Holy Spirit, I shared the story of Joseph and how God does not waste any of our suffering. As I lay on the table, God so touched the heart of the technician that she wept. I left there, too, with a clear report. How I praise God greatly for His goodness, His presence, His answers to our prayers, and His healing touch. Exodus 33:14 says, My presence shall go with thee. Indeed He went with me that day. And through His Word, He touched lives. To Him be all glory, honor, and praise!!! Alleluia!!!

Laura Simpson   6-6-15

Thought For Today

The seven names of God. These reveal Him as meeting every need of man from his lost state to the end. As you read hear the power of Almighty God through His names!

Jehovah-jireh The Lord will provide (Gen. 22:13&14)

And Abraham lifted up his eyes, and looked, and behold behind him a ram caught in a thicket by his horns: and Abraham went and took the ram, and offered him up for a burnt- offering in the stead of his son. Abraham, the father of our faith, God tested. Was he willing to give his son as his sacrifice to God? He passed the test with flying colors! At that very moment God provided the sacrifice for Abraham's offering to Him. And then we see God's provision in the ultimate sacrifice of His Son, Jesus Christ, for the way of our salvation. We must see Him, too, as the one who provides for all our needs.

Jehovah-rapha The Lord that heals

(Ex. 15:26) And said, If thou wilt diligently hearken to the voice of the Lord thy God, and do that which is right in His sight, and wilt give ear to His commandments, and keep all His statutes, I will put none of these diseases upon thee, which I have brought upon the Egyptians: for I am the Lord that healeth. When you read these words look at all the stipulations God gives for healing to come. And remember, too, the verse in the New Testament which says, by His stripes we are healed. I can testify to His healing because He has healed me. I know God doesn't always heal, but many times He does. I believe He wants us to pray with faith, standing on the promises of His Word. And I, too, believe that our physical healing is a

Laura Russell Simpson

spiritual issue. For example, I believe that nurturing bitterness and unforgiveness will lead to health problems.

Jehovah-nissi The Lord our Banner

(Ex. 17:8-15) Then came Amalek, and fought with Israel in Rephidim. And Moses said unto Joshua, Choose us out men, and go out, fight with Amalek: tomorrow I will stand on the top of the hill with the rod of God in mine hand. So Joshua did as Moses had said to him, and fought with Amalek: and Moses, Aaron, and Hur went up to the top of the hill. And it came to pass, when Moses held up his hand, that Israel prevailed: and when he let down his hand, Amalek prevailed. But Moses hands were heavy; and they took a stone, and put it under him, and he sat thereon; and Aaron and Hur stayed up his hands, the one on the one side, and the other on the other side; and his hands were steady until the going down of the sun. And Joshua discomfited Amalek and his people with the edge of the sword. And the Lord said unto Moses, Write this for a memorial in a book, and rehearse it in the ears of Joshua: for I will utterly put out the remembrance of Amalek from under heaven. And Moses built an altar and called the name of it Jehovah-nissi. For he said, Because the Lord hath sworn that the Lord will have war with Amalek from generation to generation. In the dictionary a banner is defined as a flag or ensign; a headline running across a newspaper page; a strip of cloth on a pole bearing a slogan or emblem, and a banner year is an excellent year. Remember in a war the flag/banner goes before those who fight under it. Under God, Our Banner, He goes before us fighting for us. And the victory He gives us is excellent! Significant here is the raising of the hands. The raising of hands in praise to God for the victory He gives us! Only when Moses hands were raised did Israel prevail. And don't you know how they praised Him as He gave them the victory! Let us raise our hands in praise as He goes before us to fight our battles!

Jehovah-Shalom The Lord our Peace

(Judges 6:21-24) Then the angel of the Lord put forth the end of the staff that was in his hand, and touched the flesh and the unleavened cakes; and there rose up a fire out of the rock, and consumed the flesh and the unleavened cakes. Then the angel of the Lord departed out of his sight. And when Gideon perceived that he was an angel of the Lord, Gideon said, Alas, O Lord God! For because I have seen an angel of the Lord face to face. And the Lord said unto him, Peace be unto thee; fear not: thou shalt not die. Then Gideon built an altar there unto the Lord, and called it Jehovah-shalom: unto this day it is yet in Ophrah of the Abi-excites. Gideon had just witnessed an awesome display of the power of God through the angel. He said, "I have seen an angel of the Lord face to face." God offered him peace at a moment he feared for his life. Would we not want to hear these words had we, too, like Gideon, witnessed such an awesome display of a powerful God? Well, He does offer us peace many, many times. He offers us His supernatural peace that surpasses all understanding. Jesus own Words to us, My peace I leave with you. In these Words there is something very special about God's peace. It's a peace that goes deeper than what we humanly comprehend.

Jehovah-ra-ah The Lord is my Shepherd

(Psalm 23) We are always sheep going astray. He lovingly knows we need a shepherd. The crook of His staff is always around our necks to bring us back to a safe place under His protection. And Jesus tells us He is the Good Shepherd. We are in His sheep herd never left outside for the wolves to consume. In Psalm 23 He gives us the truth of His shepherding us and also great comfort.

Jehovah-tsidkenu The Lord our Righteousness

(Jeremiah 23:6) In His days Judah shall be saved, and Israel shall dwell safely:

and this is the name whereby He shall be called, THE LORD OUR RIGHTEOUSNESS

This scripture is prophetic. It speaks of the coming restoration and conversion of Israel. For us we know that when our Father looks at us and sees that we are covered by the precious blood of His Son, He declares us righteous. The blackness of sin makes us unrighteous, but the crimson blood of Jesus makes us white as snow! We are joint heirs with Christ, so all He has is ours. And righteousness is one!

Jehovah-shammah The Lord is Present

(Ezk. 48:35) It was round about eighteen thousand measures: and the name of the city from that day shall be, The Lord Is There.

His words to His people then, and His people/us now! There is a verse which says, My presence will go with you! He says, too, He will never leave us or forsake us. We are never alone. What wonderful words from our Father who loves us dearly!

Lord (Jehovah) means Deity. Especially in covenant with His beloved chosen people, Israel.

(Ex. 19:3) And Moses went up unto God, and the Lord called unto him out of the mountain, saying, Thus shalt thou say to the house of Jacob, and tell the children of Israel; ye have seen what I did unto the Egyptians, and how I bare you on eagles' wings and brought you unto Myself.

He is their God! He is showing them how it is He who has carried them! Carried them as on eagle's wings! What beautiful words! These words are for us, too, as we are His children, too. If we have been redeemed by the blood of Jesus, we become children of God. All His promises are ours, too!

Lord God (Jehovah-Elohim) again speaks of His Deity. The Supreme Being! The One True God! The Alpha and the Omega! The

Beginning and The End! The Creator of All Things and All Men! The Lover of Our Souls! The Father of our Lord and Savior, Jesus Christ! The Omnipotent One! The Righteous Judge! Almighty God!

Let us worship Him, our Father and our God, and our Creator! Our Savior, our Lord, and our King!

Alleluia!!!

Laura Simpson   12-19-15

Joy To The World The Lord Is Come! Joy To The World He's Coming Again!!! Listening for the trumpet sound!!!

Alleluia!!!

Laura Simpson   12-13-15

Quote for the Day

Life is not measured by the breaths we take, but by the moments that take our breath away. Unknown

Comment: How many times has God taken your breath away? Alleluia!!!

About the Author

Laura Russell Simpson is in reality the ghostwriter for the one who gave her this collection of writings, namely Almighty God. She is one whose life has been dramatically changed by the power of Almighty God. At sixty-six years of age, Laura Russell Simpson was healed of a stroke she had suffered in 2014, delivered from bipolar disorder, now not diabetic, and waiting patiently and expectantly on healing of foot problems. After years of struggles through pits and prisons, like Joseph, the patriarch, God has now brought her out to an abundant life of victory and joy, no matter the circumstances. Her heart's desire is to serve the God she loves first by answering His call to share His great love for all, to share the way of salvation through His Son, Jesus Christ, and to share the power of His Word, which she highly esteems. She has shared forty-six years with her husband, Bill, thirty-nine years with her daughter, Lauran, and twenty-one years with her grandson, Josh. She resides in her hometown of Rock Hill, South Carolina. She considers herself to be greatly blessed in many, many ways by the God and Savior she loves and lovingly serves.

Printed in the United States
By Bookmasters